SKETCH BOOK

BY:
EMILY O` GORMAN
AND
HER LITTLE
COMRADES

Contents

Dedication

Thank you Acanethis, and Eyraclis, Tamara, and Buddha. You've saved my life. This book is also dedicated to those that helped me train for my careers.

Lastly, I love you, my dear wife Tammy.

Red is Anxeity

"Red and Blue Create the sky

And Yellow and Green Create the sun

Because if you remove green

You get Yellow

And if you create the

Blue with the green with

The red

And remove the green

You get red

And red is anxiety

And anxiety is a shady assetless person

And that's anxiety to Me."

-Emily

Hate Her Contradictions

Her name is

Contradiction and her pack

HATE HER

For Us- People to thrive

Her Name is Beyond The sleaze

Contradicted- the let to be in - to win

Hate Her and Her Pack

Hate Her Contradiction

Her name is

The Hypocrite

To Us Forever – Our Pact

To be Included – To be Loved

To be Intended – To love Others

To be heard never less communicate

The Maracha Man

The Man Who

Lives in my Van

He`s the van man

He`s my sleeping

Beauty

He`s my Little Maraca Man

I want to see him

Maracha Man

That Dream is All he Needs

Hi Maracha Man

Skept

This Guy

He`s Everything I want

I need

I want His Little Human Beings.

To Cuddle with Him on Christmas Eve

He`s a Soul I can`t Help but Melt

He`s Angry at me

But He has your back by under a

X-mas tree

He`s angry at me

He sees Fleas

He`s Close but closer; he needs

That kiss is all he sees

That kiss is all he needs

Closure is all he dreams

Closure is all he needs

That is why to see a soul beneath,

That's me, We.

I am his; you're His beneath

Please believe; he's the nicest thing I

Ever seen. But Not like the Guy I needed

To be with, just the guy of the Past

To be A friend.

To write in A book.

To see a letter come through

Not me and You, But I need

A friend to talk to.

When it's always Forever

I need someone to PULL ME OUT

Like, Not Bad Behavior

He's A savior

For I needed, A Favor

I needed a savior

A save Her

Not a Car, A deed, A friend

A captain Save My Hoe-In-One

To say

I disrespond to a call that surrounds

in a soul, I just need you to know it's about He inside. Ask
Him.

Because this is how he hides

I KNOW NOTHING

-YET-

But He`s I needed that Kiss

It's just a wish I could give to a soul

It's him I could give to fix a soul of a guy

Who`s always needed it

And wanted It

But I Do, And I can

Of a man, A lost Questioning

Person he and I wrote this book I

swear I had to look at the book

It was right away; you & we made

It ONE DAY Afterward, you see

He is Mine? You`re Underneath

Don`t Hide In his Chest

It's almost time to leave

Don`t You

See

I MISS YOU ALREADY

ITS AN APPRECIATION FOR "ME"

Noe for a minute, I saw him for who

He was for once & Not by the site of

His Mouth

But the back sass is what he chose

To send Down

I Think

Why is This?

It`s About to See...

ANNNDD

I'm talking about,

Does He See?

I thought He does

I needed A book

15

Train

It would have made my life

From absolute to beyond the youth,

A beautiful drive

"You went the wrong way."

That's no lie.

The Heart Evolved Train

This guy Jeremiah

He's my souls Eyes

He is a relevant theatrical guy.

Lived to through it in the faces of the ones

Corrupted, they lead it,

And they were all along pathetic

"However, I pathetically corrected it,"

To be told,

I should have left him

He is my raspberry jerry fairy tale,

Jerry Berry, my sweet apple pie,

Truly a cherry carry,

A protector, a provider,

So Gary is scary,

And also, a sweety

He's my raspberry Jerry fairytale.

Alison Wonder man, is she okay?

12/03/21

I do what he says,

Yeah yeah, that's your excuse

We, the people,

Who don't hurt other people that

Deserve the best things in life

Aren't always the one?

Who doesn't complain

Isn't that insane?

Behind the lovely – I've

Analyzed intro to paradise

They believed it seemed like a flame

Too strong for me to let go

They initiated conversate

He was stuck in a flame,

No fire is a dangerous game

He locked himself up

I don't know about this

But tough luck

Why did I not check?

In where she has been

Is she the same, or am I the one?

To push it away, ashamed

is it crazy to believe?

Is he still mad at me?

I hate to water this drift

I had to see...

I don't remember why

But they few Hella high

I believed that guy

what were you inside?

It's great

somehow, he stayed

He couldn't shake

I think

But where were you?

I thought

Because my mind was shot

All I know is that there's glitter

And its too shiny to be golden or something

He stepped away

I thought don't too much

Stay, but don't go away wilder

A little in a day

Then he stepped

In a straight face

He walked me down

Old memory lane

He a new dollar and

A new memory he made

without his collectibles

He's my collectible

He's all of a sudden

it needs to be replaced

Wear it with no brain

It's a running game boot

it's me you

Still, don't believe

You indeed

A plea Don't leave

Stay

He's so glittery I am

Swirling

Where is he, I twirling

And glittering

Interviewing, he's so

What he is

He's so

Analyzing his beaten brain

In a high up way

Where the next phase, I

Can't wait

He's gorgeous,

I can't stop

He's

There's something in the way he moves his thoughts

I can't even stop

it's NO

Ashamed

He's literally so clear to me

it was me,

who cleared the fog

He's a GOD

He cared; he was there

He needed to go ahead,

that could be seen

It sounds kinda mean

words interesting

LET ME EXPLAIN

He's a pain.

But all of a sudden

They were there

And I was happier

He let them

Cause she's set apart

It's a start, then

He stayed

Except for that day

When in the mirror

I showed no shame

He's so angry

Because I don't know

Why

he's a guy

I Can't Shake

His eyes were so on point

I pushed him away

Now I sit alone

with his shirt

On my chest

what's next

It was life

When I had to decide

It wasn't life

It was an E

Which was a sad part

The sad part

But, it was a finish

To a start

A sketch artist

Effective

Because I let myself

Get

Ineffectively discorrected

Ineffectively dis? Corrupted.

THE FIVE I's by EMILY O'Gorman

- Integrity.
- Intuition.
- Interpretation.
- Instincts.
- Importance.

Train Theory Definition: Would you jump if someone told you to hop over the track as a train is coming?

The Unrelatable/Unreliable Theory:

There are multiple waves to look at a situation that is most likely unrelated.

Gut instinct – A feeling

Gut instinct feeling – Knowing

Gut instinct conclusion – Drawing

Fact or conclusion based on what you know

Reality is to use the theory called logic.

The use of the brain means a link to all the possible scenarios.

Please Respond

To: Respond

Subject: Responsibility

From: Respect

(Please Respond)

Don't forget the FIVE I's. They mean everything to me.

The first one is called to respect yourself and love and care for others. It is called **Integrity**.

The second one is called **Intuition**, does this truly, at heart, feel right?

The next one is **Interpretation.** Hear peoples' stories and analyze all you can.

See, there is more to it.

Do you follow **Instincts?** Foolishly or gravitationally by internal marvel feelings?

And very **Important** to seek how important, the lesson can be achieved by learning.

Reply.

Forward.

Reply with an automated message.

This Is My Anti Possession Page

And the lights did show

Would you choose to see if?

The person's possessions you

Need would guarantee

You're the one that is

Underneath.

Would you [choose] seek

Your clothes off your knee

For someone else's

Eyes that see,

From a pupil of a soul

From the window of a being

That's deceiving

RETRIEVE

You're personal being

Prevention

BE above the crowd

They try ----

They aren't allowed.

      -   This is my possession

      Page: By Emile O'Gorman

Homeless Scenario Day 1

It was on that day

I was home without homeless

For good, that it was

A fight for a ride

Out of that, do you even

Bother, I just pulled that

Out of a hat, its the disguise

On the day, I entered

The nightshade's shadows

Or mmmmm

Fly away

Fly away

Flight away

Go on home now

To my cold bed

Let's keep working on the day next ahead.

Santa drinks, Santa blinks

Santa tough, tough enough

Can we please make up?

Random Words of Achievement Along The Way

A gift to be, meet us, we?

A gift to you, I'll get you…

TAKE EVERYTHING I SAW AND DO NOT WITH A GRAIN OF SALT, BUT WITH AN ENTIRE OCEAN OF' SALT PUT TOGETHER IN ONE SALT ROCK, MEANING IT'S IMPORTANT

It's a glacier of salt!

By: Emily O'Gorman

I like this book, but the spine

It needs a little tune-up.

Exposure Therapy Tool

It is to allow yourself to open your mind to the ideas that expand your mentality to the type of things you fear and how they can be perceived from a different angle by allowing yourself to see it from small steps to larger ones based on what you fear or need alone.

Hurting is not an option once you overcome challenges and realize life is getting much better without being or consuming yourself with being consumed in your thoughts to overcome the control of a livingness forever.

The Heart-Evolved Train

By Emily O' Gorman

This guy Jeremiah,

He is my train in my soul's eyes

He is a relevant theatrical guy

Has made my life, *my life*

From absolute to beyond youth

A beautiful drive

But guy

You went the wrong way

That's no lie

It was life

If I had to decide

It wasn't life but a lie

That was the sad part

But it was a finish to a start

A sketch artist's effective parte

Because I let myself get

Ineffectively dis-corrected

Lived to only throw it into the one's face, corrupted

They lead it, and they were all along pathetic

However, I pathetically corrected it

To be told,

I should've never left him be

My Rassberry jerry fairytale

jerry berry, my sweet apple pie

Truly a cherry-carry

A protector and provider

Jeremiah is Jeremiah & also a sweetie

He's been my Rassberry jerry fairytale

Alison Wonder Man: Is she okay?

Written by Emily O'Gorman

12/23/21

I do what he says

To let things defuse

Yeah, yeah, yeah, that's your excuse!

We, the people who don't hurt others

People that deserve the best things in life

Aren't always the ones that don't complain

Isn't it insane?

Behold the lovely love I've analyzed

An intro to paradise!

They believed and sought a flame

Too strong for me to let go

They initiated conversate

He was struck by a flame

Not fire, a dangerous game

He locked himself up

I don't know this

Why did I not check?

In where he has been?

Is she safe? Am I the one?

To push it away? Ashamed

Is it crazy to believe?

Is he still mad at me?

I hate to water this drift

I had to see

I don't remember why

But they flew hella high!

I believed that guy

What were you inside?

"It's great," he told

Somehow, he stayed

He couldn't shake it, I think

But where were you? I thought

Because my mind was shot

Glitter, and it's too shiny

To be golden or something

He stepped away

I thought 'don't' too much

Stay, but don't go away, wilder

A little in-a-day reminder

Then he stepped up

In a straight face

He walked me down memory lane

He's a new dollar

A new memory he made

Without his collectibles

He's my collectible

He's all of a sudden

Needing to be replaced

Wear it with no brain

It's a running game

It's me & you

Still don't believe you indeed

A plea, don't leave

Stay

He's so glittery

I am swirling

Where is he? I twirling

And oh so glittery

Intertwining, he's so…

What is he?

He's so…

Analyzing his freakin brain!

In a high-up way,
Where's the next phase,
I Can't wait.

He's gorgeous. I can't stop.
There's something in the
Way he moves his thoughts.

I can't even stop.
It's No
Ashame

He's literally so clear to me.
It was me,

Who cleared the fog.

He's a GOD.
He cared. He was there.

He needed a head,
That could be seen.
It sounds kind of mean.

Words interesting,
LET ME EXPLAIN.
He's a pain.

But all of a sudden,
They were there,
And I was happier.

He let theirs,
Cause she's set part.
It's a start,
Then he stayed.

Except that Day.

When in the mirror,

I showed No Shame.

And He's so angry,

Because don't know

Why

He's a guy.

I can't shake.

His eyes were so on point.

I pushed him away.

Now I sit alone,

With his shirt

On my chest

What's Next.

Please Respond

TO: Respond Subject: Responsibility From: Respect

(Please Respond)

Don't Forget the FIVE I'S. They mean everything to me. The First one is called to respect yourself & love and care for others it's called Integrity. The second one is called Intuition. Does this feel right at heart? The next one is Interpretation. Hear people's Stories and analyze all you can, and there's more to it. Do You Follow Instincts? By your internal manual feelings? And very important to seek what lesson can be achieved by learning.

Replay

Forward

Reply with an automated message.

A Perfectionist

When you,

choose to sit

it out

to make another

Person happy.

The Five I's

By Mily o Ijorman

1. Integrity

2. Intention

3. Interpretation

4. Institics

5. Importance

DE-CODE! TO PROCESS!

TREN Theory Definition- IF SOMEONE TOLD You To
Hop over the tracks. As a train is coming WOULD You Do
it?

The Unreliable theory-There are multiple to look at a situation that are or are most likely on related.

Gut instinct - A Feeling

Gut instinct Feeling-knowing

Gut instinct conclusion- coming to

Gut instinct Knowledge- Drawing Fact or conclusion based on what you know

Reality is to use the theory called Logic.

In A High Up Way

In a high-up way
Where's the next phase?
I Can't wait.

He's gorgeous, I can't stop.
There's something in
The way he moves his thoughts.

I can't even stop.
It's no shame.

He's literally so clear to me.
It was me, who
Cleared the fog

He's a GOD
He cared. He was there

He needed a head,
That could be seen

It sounds kinda mean

Words interesting
LET ME EXPLAIN
He's a pain.

But all of a sudden
They were there
And I was happier

He let theirs
Cause she's set part
It's a start, then
He stayed.

Except that Day.
When in the mirror
I showed No Shame.

And He's so angry.
Because I don't know
Why

He's a guy.
I can't shake it.

His eyes were so on point.
I pushed him away.

Now, I sit alone.
With his shirt
On my chest
What's Next

It was life if

I had to
Decide
It wasn't LIFE

(it was an E) That was the sad part

The Sad part

But, it was a finish to a start.

A Sketch Artist.

EFFECTIVE

Because I let myself

Bet

Ineffectively Discorrected

IN EFFECTIVELY

DIS-CORRUPTED

Can you believe the person underneath was him and me –
We?

Please Respond

TO: Respond Subject: Responsibility From Respect

(Please Respond)

Don't Forget the FIVE I'S. They mean everything to me.
The First one is called to respect yourself & love and care
for others. It is called integrity. The second one is called
Intuition. Does this at heart feel right? The next is
interpretation, hearing people's Stories, and analyzing all
you can. Sex, and there's more to it. Do You Follow
instincts Footy or gravitationally by your internal manual
Feelings? And very importantly, seek How important
lessons can be achieved by learning.

Replay

Forward

Reply with an automated message.

Be Still

When you

choose to sit

it out

to make another

Person happy

The Five I's

By Miley o Ijorman

1. Integrity
2. Intention
3. Interpretation
4. Institics
5. importance

DE-CODE! TO PROCESS!

TREN Theory Definition- IF SOMEONE TUID YOU TO

hop over the tracks. As a train is coming, WOULD You Do

it?

The unreliable theory is multiple to look at situations that are or are most likely related.

Gut instinct - A Feeling

Gut instinct Feeling-knowing

Gut instinct conclusion- coming to

Gut instinct Knowledge- Drawing Facts or conclusions based on what you know

Reality is to use the theory called logic.

My possession page

AND the lights DID show. Would you choose to see if the person's possessions you need would guarantee you're the one that is underneath?

Would you [choose] to seek your clothes off your knee for someone else's eyes that see,

From a pupil of a soul from the window of a being that's diving
RETRIEVE
You're personal being
PREVENTION
BE ABOVE THE word
They try _ _ _ _
They aren't allowed.

Homeless Scenario #2

It was on that day.

I was home without being homeless.

For Good, that night, it was

A fight for a ride.

Out of that, do you even

Bother, I just pulled that

Out of a hat, HS the Disguise

of the day I entered

the nightshade shadows

Or hmm hmm

    Fly away

    Fly Away

    FLIGHT AWAY.

Go on home. How

To my cold bed

Let's keep working the day ahead.

Santa drinks, Santa Blinks,

Santa's tough, tough enough

Can we please make up?

Please Help

A gift to be, meet us, we?

A gift to you, I'll get you…

TAKE EVERYTHING I SAY AND DO NOT WITH A
GRAIN OF SALT BUT WITH AN ENTIRE OCEAN OF
ROCK, MEANING IT'S IMPORTANT

It's a glacier of salt!

-By: Emily O'Gorman

I LIKE THIS BOOK< BUT THE SPIRE NEEDS A
LITTLE TUNE-UP.

Exposure therapy tool

It is to allow yourself to open your mind to the ideas that expand your mentality to the type of things you fear and how they can be perceived from a different angle by allowing yourself to see it from small steps to larger ones based on what you fear or need alone. Hurting is not an option once you overcome challenges & realize life is getting much better without being or consuming yourself with being consumed in your thoughts to overcome the control of a livingness forever.

Lamars Bedtime Story

3 pigs made a house

Straw, Brick, and Hay!

A coyote-Wolf

Came to eat their

Porridge & look through their windows

Meanwhile, he did blow their house down with the straw

and Hay too.

[The coyote built the house with the Hay]

The two pigs ran to the house made of brick.

Meanwhile, a human was shot.

The coyote and the whole coyote were on his back

The pigs looked out the window to see the hunter, the

coyote over

His shoulder and the pigs said

"That shit was good, but he got what he deserved."

Not By: But of a good friend, Emily, by Lamar and

reiterated to show the truth.

More Achievements

If you realize

You may pour fries

Fries or potatoes

Who knows, no's.

Who knows.

To feel the green man in your presence

On the 19th of November to the 3rd of February.

5 days in 8. 2x4 = 84

Spring lies on April 29th

It's not about unrealizing - it's about the program

Just try – if not, go back.

Let's connect; you're in the slums.

I need one, do you?

I need a friend too. I miss you.

Let's not trade, it is not safe

No longer safe 9,001,559

Let's move out of reach. To catch a fish slipping, now let's eat.

#1 Santa a claws

#2 Santa a paws

#1 + #2 Santa pause (with #1 & #2)

Wha... Santa Draws

Santa will applause

Santa says, your good

Santa says you're fried

Good Luck, Then

Yours

Hired.

Magical dots?

Why can I see magic, biological bacteria?

Somewhere between March-May 2021

I can lend you a helping hand, fool of surprises.

Ask-Literal?

Ring Ring

Mom, will you answer the phone?

No?

Why won't Dad answer the phone?

He's a maniac.

Healthy Advice

Keep living things alive, Fed, Healthy, and, more importantly, educated and knowledgeable for the sake that all Children deserve a life that is protected, not de-railed or convinced that they should CHAIN or unchain.

Did Into My Cereal Bowl
You may learn that we love each concoction of Well-rounded individualistic contribution to the Universe and its capabilities completed to ensure healing of Brain Food is considered and interpreted in a way that is analyzed and except regarding the work a read for the living things that derive from within, knowledge within to be known the contributors and the accepted individuals.

All that remains until after death 3 Desperation is the ability to bring back the original plan. What's the original plan?
Explain this: where did it go?
It's beautiful, Despicable, achievable. Where did it go?

Inside Of Your Own Hide
Atheist Sees It Belongs

TO INTERFERE FROM A BEYOND & It was gone

To LEAD a Life Above

He was hypnotized & it's gone

To go get Advice from

To Lie to ease a mind

To know what's on the outside, An Atheist secs it Belongs

Sprinkle it on a hyena

Awaiting a prey an attack an understanding a burden

An atheist says it belongs

An atheist sees it as belonging to standing the Forces to

what a then an atheist sees it belongs.

An atheist sees it Belongs and then asks to be gone.

Only a little burden to be told I'll bet you out of that Rabbit

Fake habitat

You call, on wait, you're my HOME homie.

The Princess And The Stubborn Princes

It's about a princess.

That bets everything she wants

One is entirely made of ink. One is entirely made of paper.

They coincide and collaborate.

They want to make [a great] poetry

ONLY when they try

ONE only comes up with ink

All over the paper

The other gets a paper.

Filled with INK

So what Do they Do

They go to the stubborn.

Who makes great POETRY?

Why,

Because,

They know how to control their hands.

Learn,

About my raspberry jerry FAIRYTABLE.

It's about a prices that gets Everything She wants

Eventually… in a timely manner on point, quick as it
seems, learn about the
RASPBERRY JERRY
FAIRYTALE
QUICK, ON Points, AS FAST AS IT SEEMS.

Discoveries

Where are they? Are they even here?

I feel his presence, but he doesn't speak up. YOU NEED
TO SEE THIS:

Dinosaur urine equals penicillin.

Why?

Let's never get killed.

But I have something

Better

Just wait and see

"HA HA HA – says the alien flea

"But Wait, let's make it altered."

Let me tell you a story:

I got this intense feeling. I thought it was the tomato plant-
deadly nightshade.

Said," Please, can I rip out? Can I now? What happens

When the plant is ripped out.

Tomatoes flourished and thanked me.

Come To Please - Please Heal

To hide in a moleskin notebook Diary

It is like looking into a predator's eyes so small you see a ball in the eyes.

Quickens, sweet, Defeat
To see it mold process, then foretold

Come clean, or you'll be mean.

To see a course in action

To figure the sides
Ones set aside

Alleviate the pain. You will refrain from speaking.

Use a set of Lallvlations.

Ask for help

Live like tomorrow, knowing it never was.

Motivation to seek out love for yourself.

To Feel it float away, speak, and communicate.

NEVER FALL, NEVER FATE TWO Complete, to contemplate.

They escaped the blood diamond game

Get a person on your side. Drop and please abide, then escape the Blood Diamond gang.

Not a gang of violence, a gang-free
Better without the Diamonds
Where we are not in need

To be told by some people who truly believed in the ability to see the corruptors (tions) beneath the lines no longer let it define the needs of those who seemed to be among the top-of-the-scenes

To: the people who were able to be a part of the non-FALSE storytelling that influenced many about coming together to use our brains to ensure we give a chance to be not in pain but a step forward to a gathering pain.

To Process MEANS:

The process is the most important thing you'll ever do to determine a choice. It is allowing yourself or a person to think about things from the intricate simple to the problems at stake. The best and the worst things to consider and how it allows you to think it through and the effects based on what you know or not know yet.

The hardest thing to consider is the best you may imagine to get to the route.

Beginning and End

For the concretion that all kids deserve a life that is not derailed or convinced that they should chain or unchain or derail.

ONE ON ONE PROGRESS

ONE-ON-ONE PROGRESS IS TO BE VALIDATED
AND AWARDED FOR HARD WORK IN A
NATURALISTIC WAY THAT TEACHES the value of a
person and who they can be at any given time with
EFFORTS that exceed and limits, with help, can be no
longer, as long as a person sets for their life is to care about
themselves and their work and not get stick with things that
hold them back
IF THEY CARE TO MAKE THOSE CHANGES

Have you sinned?

Have you sinned?

What is sin? It's a mix-up of LIES

They,

Are mistakes or things you have improvised from

The mind.

Who are you INSIDE?

They say as their (sore/ sour)

Hearts abide! They say!

Dis- Collide! I say!

Don't read into no lies; you stink, and I can't stand when

you pridefully whine.

It's what I needed, they say.

I say live up to your own standards

No LIE. Hold each other

Up and Decide which to cry

To

Inflict your set of eyes with.

My heart goes out to you

PTSD is a killer, or can we talk about it together? Mental
internal interpretation
FOR US/ FOR BETTER INSTEAD OF LACK OF FOR
EVERS.
Mind trips and physical abusers
Mentally USERS
Don't abuse "HER"

Breakups are hard

Don't let this fall.

Reverse

Regroup

Cooperate

I like you

I like you A lot

He cared and let it.

Don't care

You messed up

And I loved (love) him

Talk to me

By the way

This really

Needs a fix

I'm going for you

Lease

Feet Vs. Shoe Scenario

If you found twenty $ on the ground
Would you choose
To seek
Out a thrift store to surprise
Twenty or so people with a pair of shoes,
Said a homeless man to you
"I have a valid size." I have the same as yours."
Or would you choose
To see a store owner
In need of a valuable
Penny to replace
A collection of rubber
Souls with a new old
Box in the back of the store.

To take time out?
To actually change their
Lives by living a dollar to
A pair of shoes
Of many multiple kinds
Specifically, what is your size?

How far away are you now?

A longing to be seen---

And heard.

So what

You're saying

THE TEARS WERE REAL

To not know

A future

Ever, even

Is it ever available?

You got this

You got this.

Respectable.
She should respect my dis.
To her, she shall leave.
To be seen later, maybe
Not too SELFISHLY
Use me not for my best
Interest, or was a test
Implied or implemented to
See If How Could, I leave.
On the terms of me, we, us.
Please. Trust it. Happy?
Thing rationally.
Basic human decency
Using moralistic value
And logic.

ESENTIALLY, DO YOU HURT YOURSELF OR
OTHERS?

IN THE END.

-Please explain it-

To me, Emily

From us to/ from you.

He's my Raspberry Jeremiah FAIRYTALE

With spoons in my head

However, you roll.

Be unique

That's my type of people

Creativity you speak

Contemplate everything

Use your brain

Communication is key

Put in effort

Analyze everything, but always be sweet in your heart

And sing, sing, sing

From the effects to a new start

An exciting adventure to excel

We are humans who made mistakes, embrace

Each other's learning and continue an

Intuitive, instinctual, interpretive way.

To the beginning

To The End
From and again
To a beginning

THE ENDING
Welcoming freedom
Within

Free to Within

Freed-IN

And she's a good pick-out

And she's a good pick-out.

For you, she loves you.

Too, we see it.

I like to make people proud.

Of me, and

I don't like to

Make people proud of me

And I don't like to make people

I love, look dump,

Unless they already do & ill

Have the backs

Of the ones I site

With for logic

Not the feeling inside an

Emotional skew or "fakeness"

I like to be genuine of

How I see it. And I'll tell you why

I had you so wondersome

He had a bi-winning attitude

But not bi-polar

I didn't know yet, did I?

All I knew when I realized

Finally

Will I make him proud?

Now-where were you for me?

Be with you now.

A Deadend-less just to be anxious?

Dis-die what

Is he told him

They killed his social life.

After they brought him

To the top, for reasons

Previously talked about maybe,

To squash the shit out of me

They didn't

Followed for a laugh.

Or something, all I know

Is peer pressure a silent killer?

Sketched.

To gain the answers to a test?

Tough, but now it can be

I hated what I did to him because

They see him. I'm right for you.

It makes me feel proud knowing

I'm excepted from the

BEST FRIENDS OF THE BEST MAN IN MY LIFE.

Because they see interest

To look out for a Homie

Her name is a contradiction, and her pack

Her name is a contradiction, and her pack

HATE HER

FOR US-People to thrive

Her name is beyond- the sleaze

Contradicted-the lets to bein-town.

To us forever- to be loved

To be included, be loved

To be intended-to love others

To be heard- never less communicate

Hate her and her pack

Hate her contradiction

Her name is the hypocrites

The Marachaman

This man who

Live in my van

He's the van man

He's my sleeping beauty

He's my little maraca man

I want to see him

Manana man

That Dream is all they need.

Hi Marachaman

-He's still asleep.

Red and Blue create the sky

"Red and Blue create the sky
And Yellow and Green create the sun

Because if you remove green
You get Yellow
And if you create the
Blue with the green with the Red
Remove the green
You get red
Red is anxiety
And anxiety is a shady-asset less person
And that's anxiety time."

Sketch

This guy Jeremiah,
He's everything I want I need

I want his little human beings. To
Cuddle with him on Chrisman eve
He's a soul I can't help but melt

He's angry @ me.
But He's have your back by me under a
X-mas trees.
He is angry at me.
He sees Fleas
He's close, but closer he needs
That kiss is all He sees
That kiss is all He needs
Closure is all he dreams of. He needs

That's why to see a soul beneath,
That's me, <u>we</u>.
I am his. You're his beneath

Please believe, He's the nicest thing I
Ever seen. But not Like, I needed
To be with, just the guy of the
Past, to be a friend. To write in a book

Why is this?

It's about seen...

ANNNDD

I'm talking, but Does he see?

I thought He does
I needed A Book

But it's a problem,
Probably Beyond "me?"

I think so FAR, you see you made it
With me, but it is Us and Him

And He wrote back to MD.

Please! Tell me all
It was a wild trip up
How we (balled) met
But I didn't get to tell him himself-less
Did I?

To see a letter come through
Not ME AND YOU, But I need
A friend to talk to.

When it's always FOREVERS
I need someone to pull me out.
Like, not Bad behavior
He's a savior
For I Needed A Favor
I need a Savior to save her
Not a car, a deed, a friend
A caption save my Hoe-IN-ONE
To say
I Disrespond to a call that surrounds
In a soul, I just need you to know its
When he gets inside, ask him
Because this is how he hides
I KNOW NOTHING
-YET-

But He's I needed that kiss
It's just a wish. I wish I could give to a soul

It's him I could give to fix the soul of a guy
Who's always needed it?

And wanted it.

But I do, and I can

Of a man, a lost questioning
The person he and I wrote this book, I
Swear I had to look at the book
It was Right away. You & I made
It's ONE DAY Afterword, you see
HE IS MINE; you're underneath

Don't Hide in his chest.
It's almost time to leave.
Don't you Swear?

I miss you already.
It's An Appreciation for "M"

Now, for a minute, I saw him. For who
He was, for once & Not by the site of
His mouth

But the backs ass is what he chose
To send down
I think.

How we came to forever be to:
ME AND that Guy

And his silly little soul

ID Always Love You

But

Why is His Head Closed out

It's
But said his past
Is she still around?
And that. Guy?
As we Shook, He shook His
Head
(shivered)

Not A Mess

To hear from him now,

Forever

I miss you, friend.

I hope to see you again now

He's nice

Ask him

He said nothing like seeing inside of a man

To his past Self

As a person

OH NO! It's All Chewed.

He says, then he
Plays
But he's happy, and we
Can't complain

He's perfect
Don't ever let him escape
Or let it not go away

Please talk to me and
Tell me to listen
So, we continue to listen
In a glittery fateish
Collabor-appreciation
Without a system

For all the days
From the ones who can make

In this paradise of dreams
We heard he was once the way.
Is leaving it at that okay?

Red is anxiety

By Emily O'Gorman

…and red is anxiety…

…and red is anxiety…

…and red is anxiety…

A liar once asked me, to my knowledge, if I believed

It would never be true. A once

A sinister person saw redas

Energetic and calm, and I did too, once

Instead of seeing red, she was wrong

All along.

A shady Asset person

Once told me

…and red is anxiety…

…and red is anxiety…

…and red is anxiety…

And that's anxiety to me.

The Homeless Shoe

Scenario Number one

It was on that day I was homeless for a fight for a ride.
Good that night it was. Outa that do you even bother I just
pulled that outa A hat it's the disguise of the day I entered
the night Shadow
OR:

Hmm hm hmmm

Fly away

Fly away?

Flight away

Off to work the day ahead, answers in BED to my COID
By: Emily O' Gorman

[EO] Include ELECTRONIC SINITURE HERE.

Who saw, said I, A friend.
In his past

Is she Fat?
I wanted to tell him…

To see in the End.

What He got to be with

He got me.

For your life, it was crazy.
The demand,
Maybe needed to see

Ask "Me"

That's the whole story, Except one little thing
Wasn't he here to see this?
It's like he was Blank, But One thing
I question

What's that you want me to say?

Live: A Guilty Freer Lyfestyle guideline

With these things around you, it is encouraged that people process and think things through to ensure that the correct by your heart feels like a good, best option and choice or for a progressive star at the present moment for every second of every day that nothing is a tree every second of every day that nothing is a true fail it may ensure a by your heart only a mistake.

If you try to the best of your:

#1 CAPABILITY- How much you can handle the knowledge to know, you deserve breaks and to push to try and continue to the best of this capability without pushing yourself so hard you reach a limit of failure or giving up.

#2 Knowledge LEVEL- How much you know or have learned and utilized that knowledge for perspectives of experiences or to get things done using logic, questioning everything, does this make sense, level of importance.

#3 Experience much you've acquired in your past to determine your present or what you're presented with/ of to be included in your knowledge level or understanding of what you're trying to do.

#4 Abilities- your talents and the things you're capable of doing within who you are and what you know to make things happen based on your knowledge of the abilities you have or have learned from people or yourself or within. What you're good at essentially and incorporating it in.

#5 Education level- what you've learned and have been taught up to the point and level in which you are at. This doesn't mean or have to mean you are at the same level as everyone around you or your age. Internalize & connect

To OBTAIN HAPPYNESS And
Process your life.

Testimonial Fear, I hear, and I pass through:

Testimonial Fear, I hear, and I pass

through: By Emily

It's the Planet Man. I'll give it a bowl

All get you out of the hole a whole up

I like cola, I like soda, sode-up

Jokes up. I love tequila, but I Don't

Not tequila, show up, I'm getting

Mad money, yo, let's go get more

I'm running the show, Bro,

BTW you're a hoe-but I love you

Oh so dear, yes dear, you need to go. I'm a little bit of a

weight

(wait?)…

What's that I was supposed to say

Oh yeah (shirred)

"Hey."

At least, "Are you okay?"

Blockages By: Em

I initiated a conversation.

All bets aside, do I dare to

Hide, let's search, let's find, please

Tell me again so I don't hide.

Not even a goodbye, but wait!

I was in it to be there; they

Told me don't even go there (bother)

We need you to see, focus girl

We are in it for you to succeed

Though we are all in need, we all   -

Have to feed. Our brains are one

Within where we all Fit in a place

Of our own, I miss this. I love

Your kind, too. I'm just slipping

Because wait, hold up, where's the

Vodka, let's focus on not only

Us, that's can I get a plus… or

Something? I miss you, folks & lets

Initiate, they say, now I'm in a better pays

Rabbit hole, not for show.

c42cf230-bf90-429e-a016-2ea39ef6f20fR01